Decorative Birds
Stained Glass Pattern Book

LINDA DANIELS

DOVER PUBLICATIONS, INC., New York

Published in Canada by General Publishing Company, Ltd., 30 Lesmill Road, Don Mills, Toronto, Ontario.
Published in the United Kingdom by Constable and Company, Ltd., 3 The Lanchesters, 162–164 Fulham Palace Road, London W6 9ER.

Decorative Birds Stained Glass Pattern Book is a new work, first published by Dover Publications, Inc., in 1992.

DOVER *Pictorial Archive* SERIES

Manufactured in the United States of America
Dover Publications, Inc., 31 East 2nd Street, Mineola, N.Y. 11501

Library of Congress Cataloging-in-Publication Data

Daniels, Linda.
    Decorative birds stained glass pattern book / Linda Daniels.
        p.   cm. — (Dover pictorial archive series)
    ISBN 0-486-27267-2 (pbk.)
    1. Glass painting and staining—Patterns.   2. Birds in art.   I. Title.   II. Series.
NK5305.D36   1992
748.5′022′2—dc20   92-14480
                                                                                             CIP

PUBLISHER'S NOTE

Among the approximately nine thousand species of birds are some of the most dazzling creatures on earth. And the appeal of these brilliantly colored birds is doubled when they are featured in stained glass crafts projects such as those you can fashion from these 74 designs by artist Linda Daniels.

A selection of different shapes and patterns of varying degrees of complexity are included. They may be suitably enlarged or reduced for different types of projects.

Naturally, given their spectacular coloration, birds of the tropics predominate: Birds of Paradise, Racquet-tailed Kingfisher, Peacocks, Hummingbirds, Toucans and especially Parrots and their relatives, including Cockatoos, Macaws and Lovebirds. But there are also many colorful birds of cooler and even frigid regions: Mandarin Duck, Manchurian Crane, Raven, Cardinal, Swans, Penguins and many more.

This collection of patterns is intended as a supplement to stained glass instruction books (such as *Stained Glass Craft* by J. A. F. Divine and G. Blachford, Dover Publications, Inc., 0-486-22812-6). All materials needed, including general instructions and tools for beginners, can usually be purchased from local craft and hobby stores listed in your Yellow Pages.

Fischer's Lovebirds

Mandarin Duck

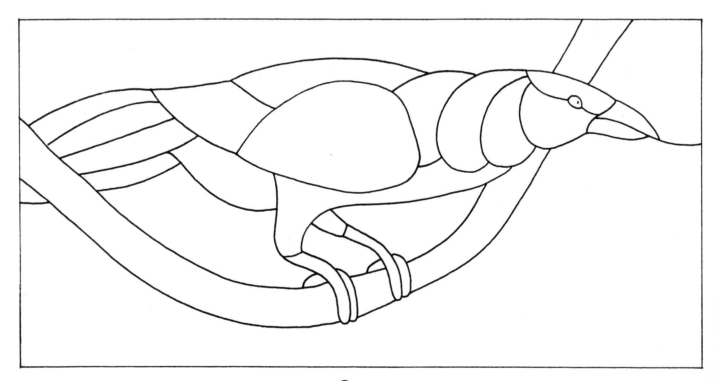

Raven

Snowy Owl

Manchurian Crane

Cockatoo

Peacock

Quail

Canary

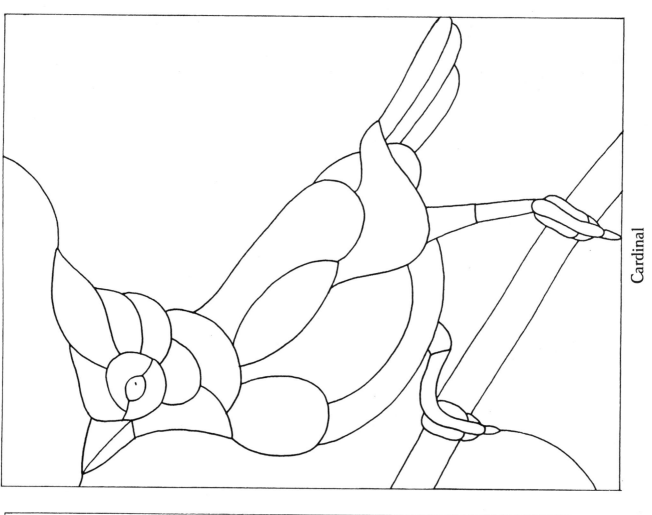

Cardinal

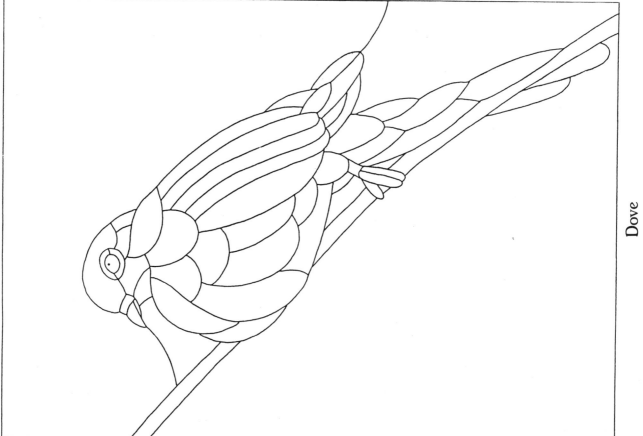

Dove

8

Crane

Peach-faced Lovebird

Gouldian Finches

Eagle

Hummingbird

Moluccan Cockatoo

Sulphur-crested Cockatoo

13

Penguins

Quetzal

Toucan

Toucan

Duckling

Snow Pheasant

Pheasant

Macaw

White-bellied Caique

Swans

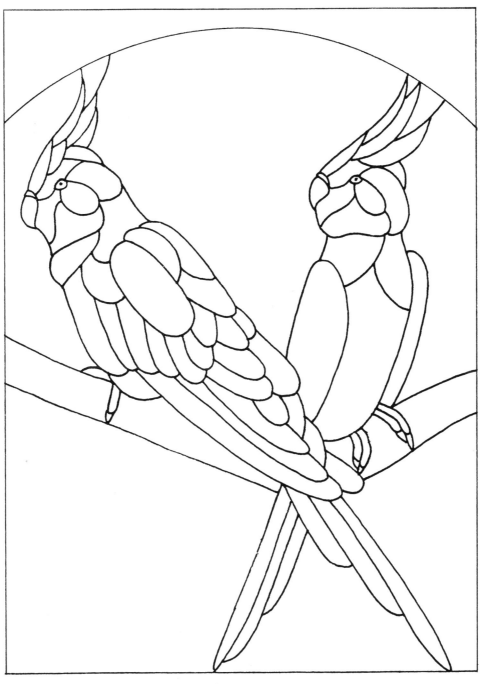

Cockatiels

Black Sickle-billed Bird of Paradise

Bluebirds

Bluebird

Hummingbird

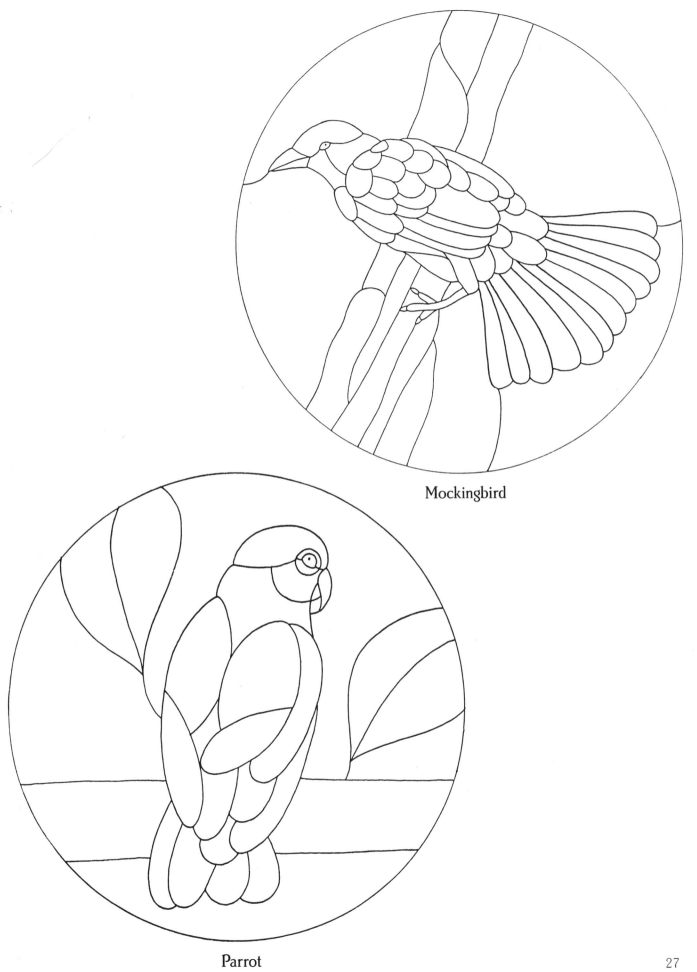

Mockingbird

Parrot

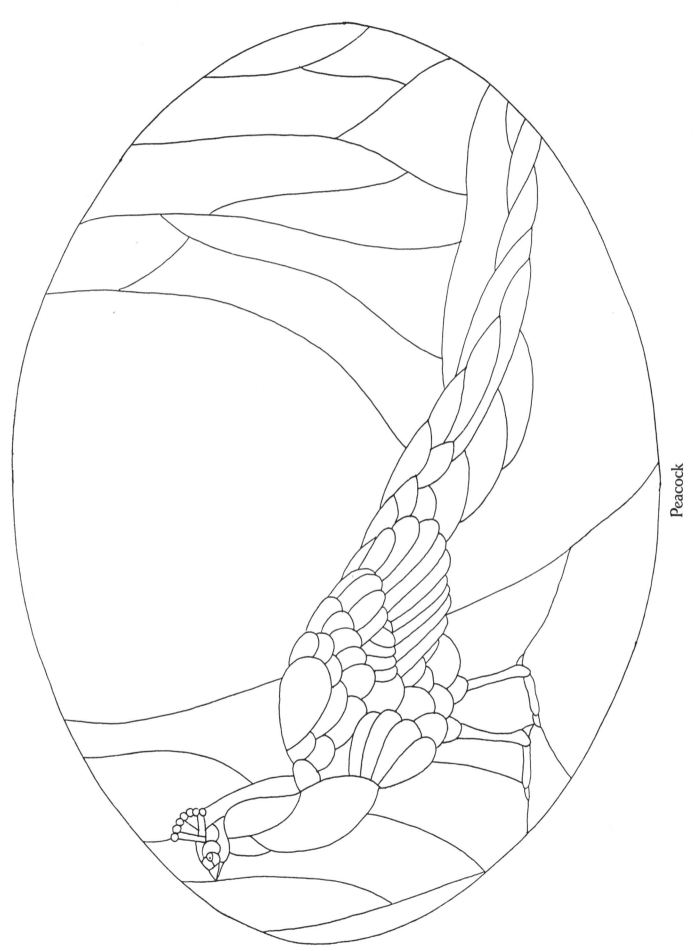

Peacock

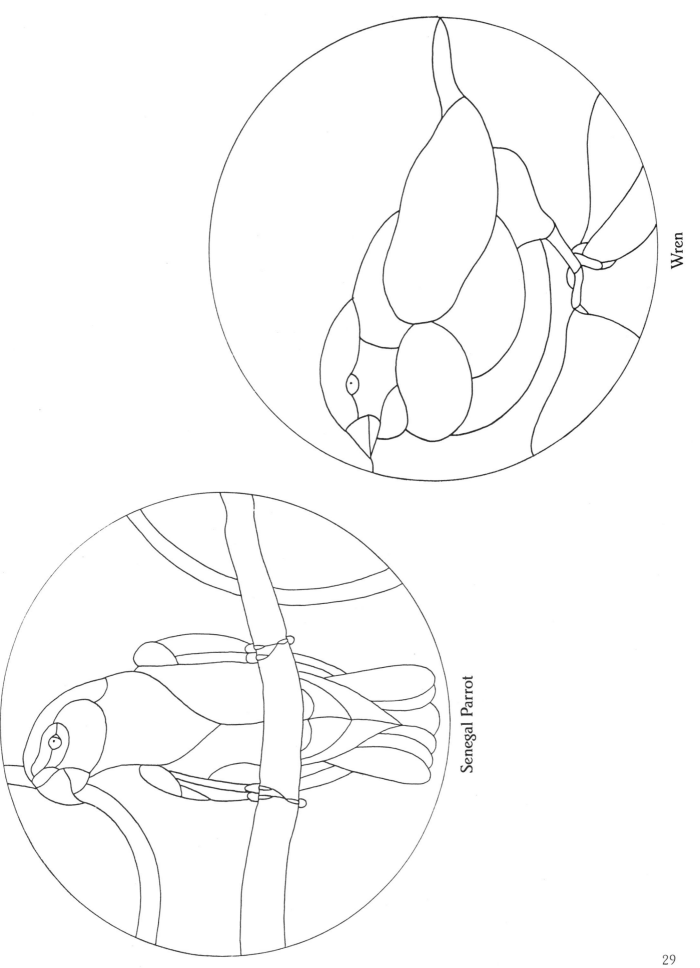

Wren

Senegal Parrot

Swan

Pheasant

Parrots

Ducks

Emperor of Germany's Bird of Paradise

Peacock

Parakeet

Eagle

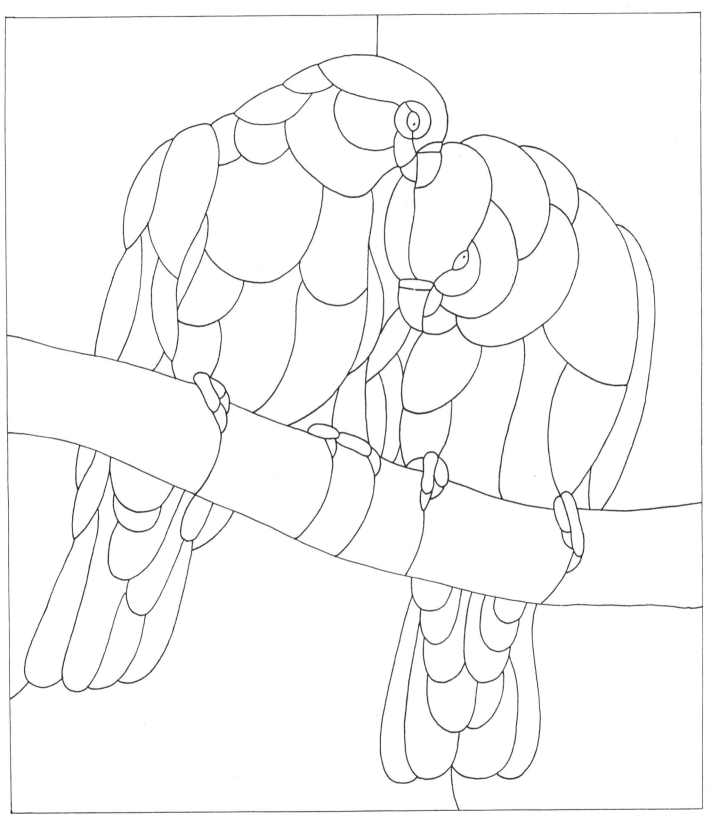

Parrots

Parrots

Gouldian Finches

Ring-necked Parakeet

Parrot

Toucan

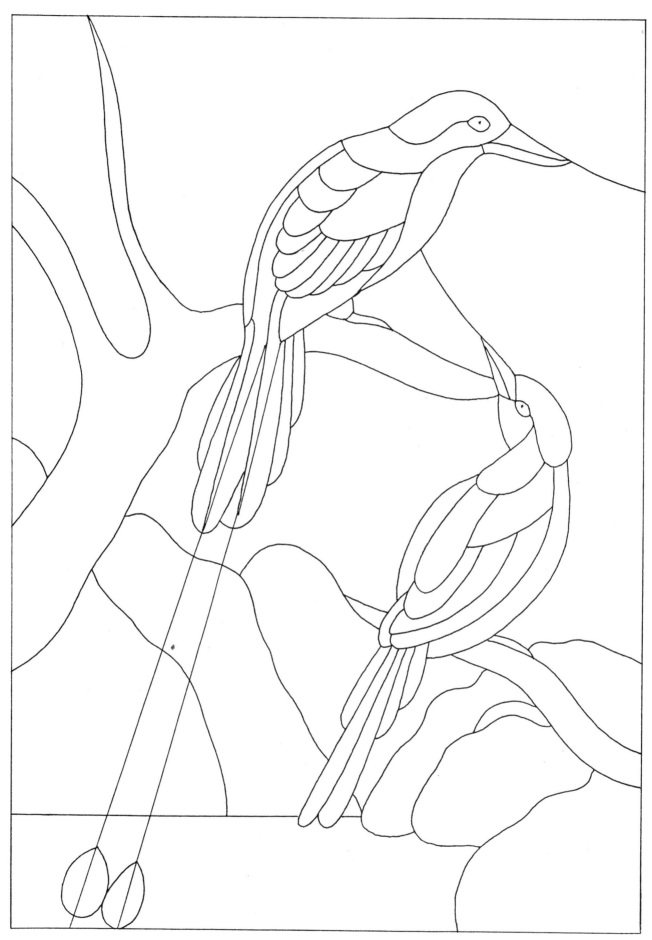

Racquet-tailed Kingfisher

Cockatiel

Cranes

Parrots

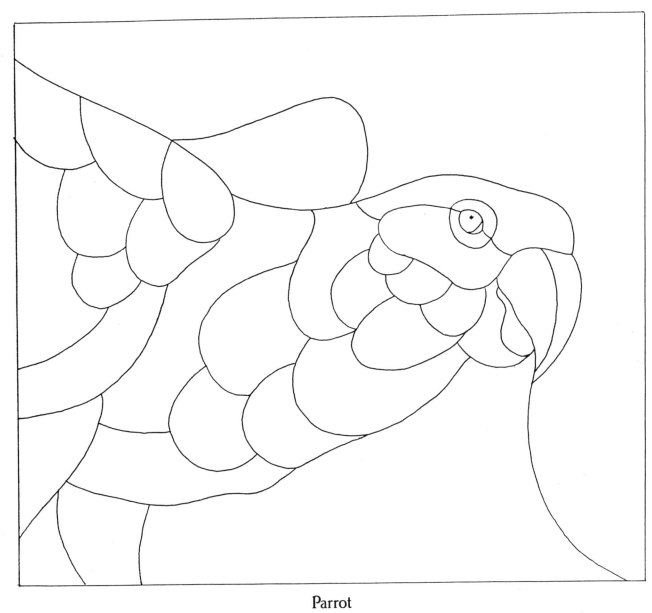

Parrot

Peacock

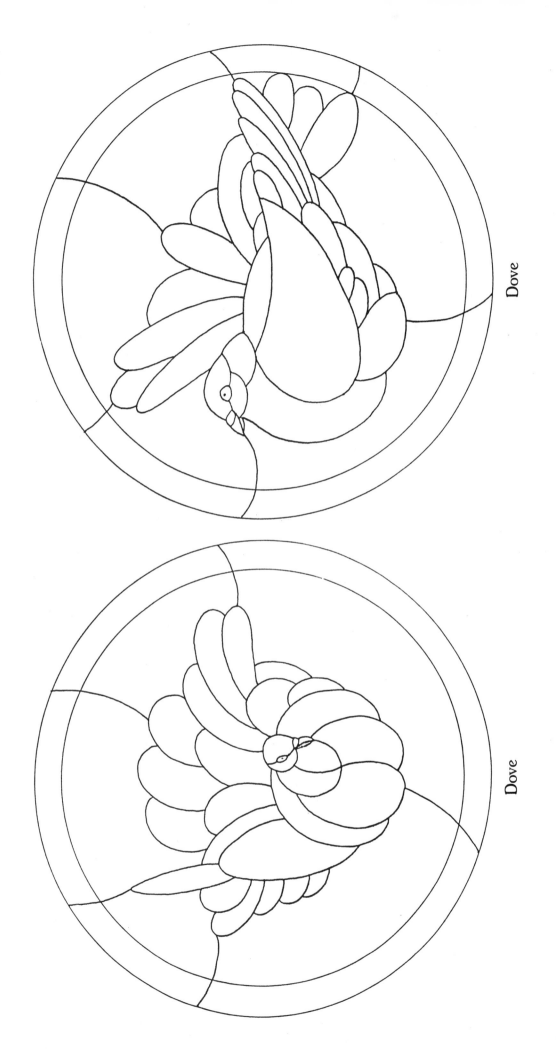

Dove

Dove

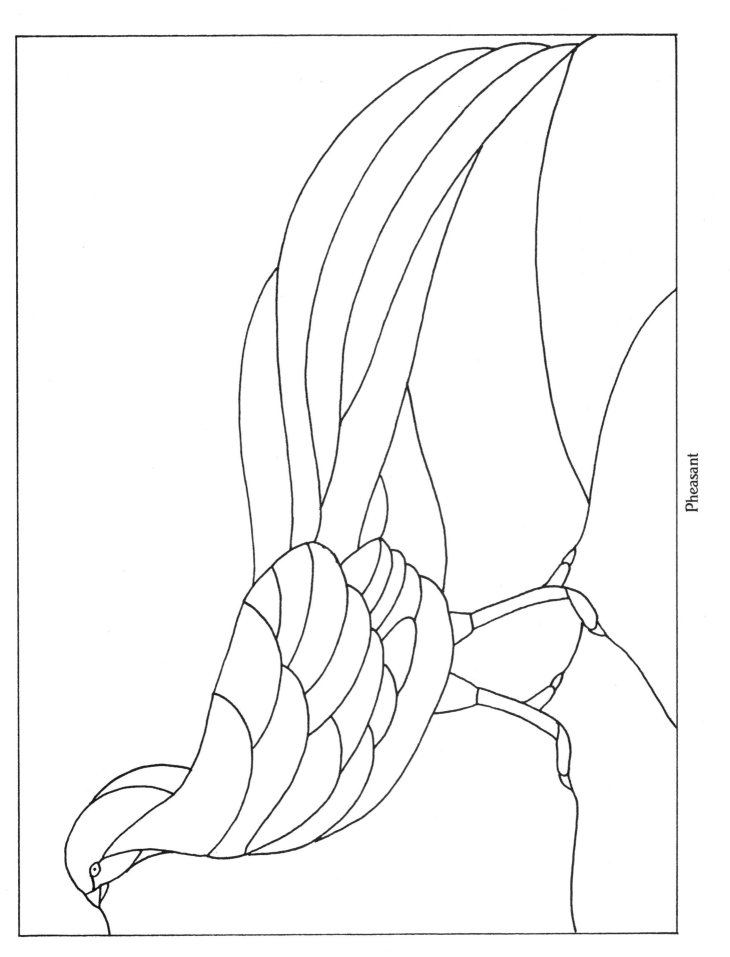

Pheasant

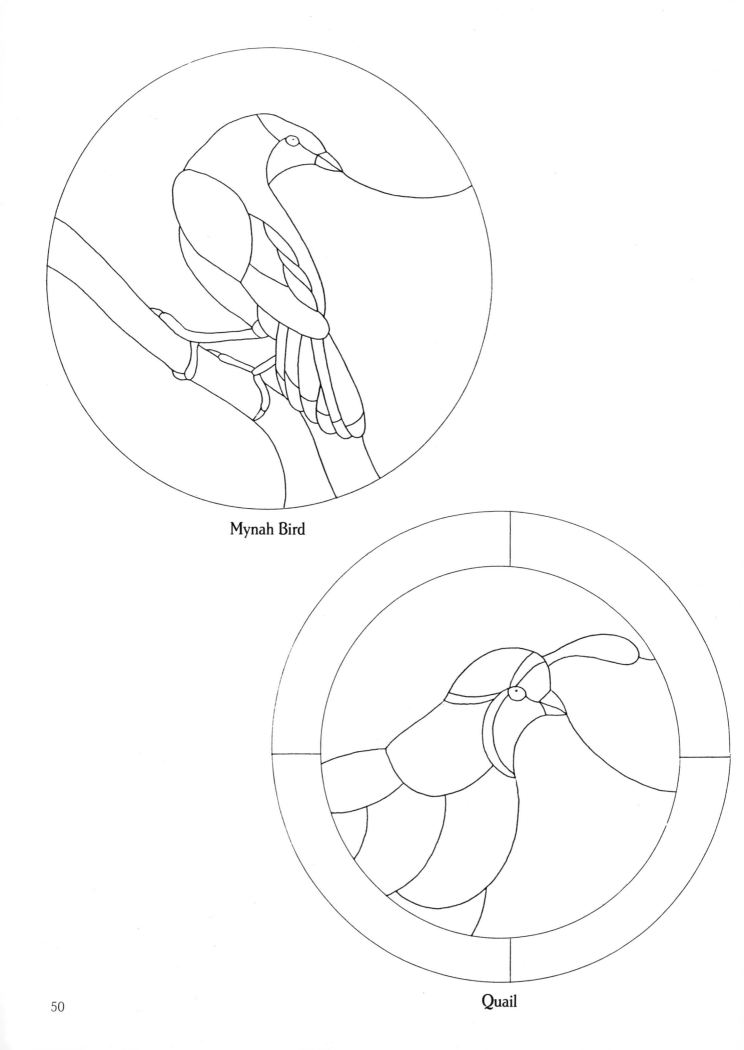

Mynah Bird

Quail

Masked Lovebird

Greenland Falcon

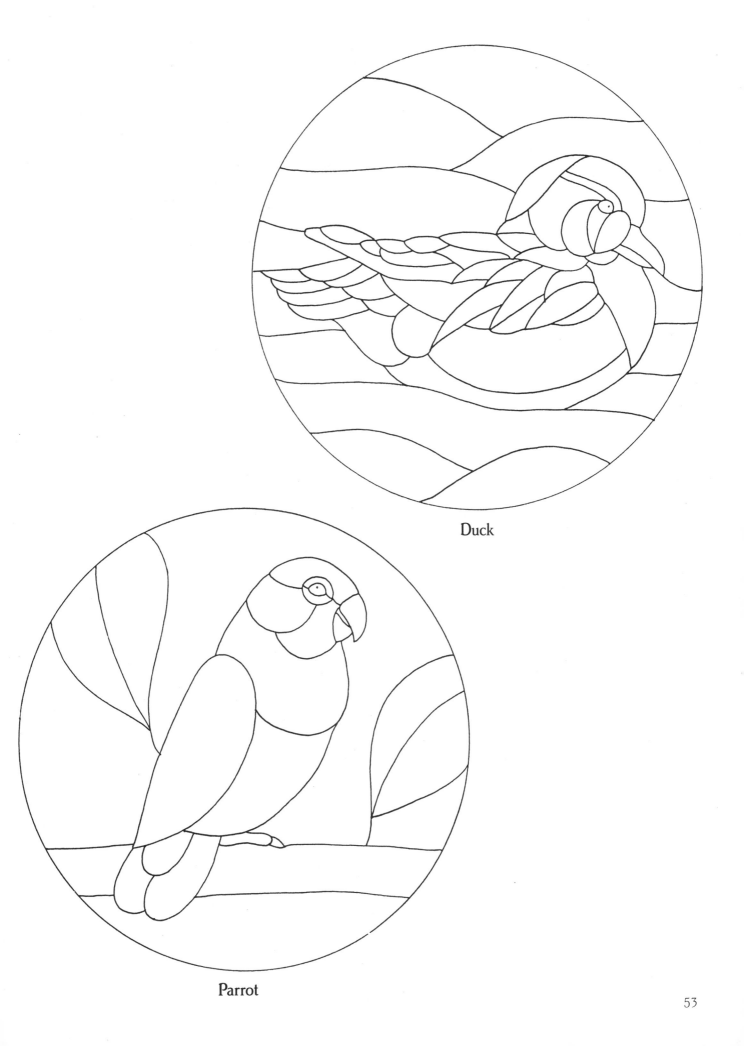

Duck

Parrot

Pigeon

Macaws

Peach-faced Lovebirds

Black-headed Gouldian Finch

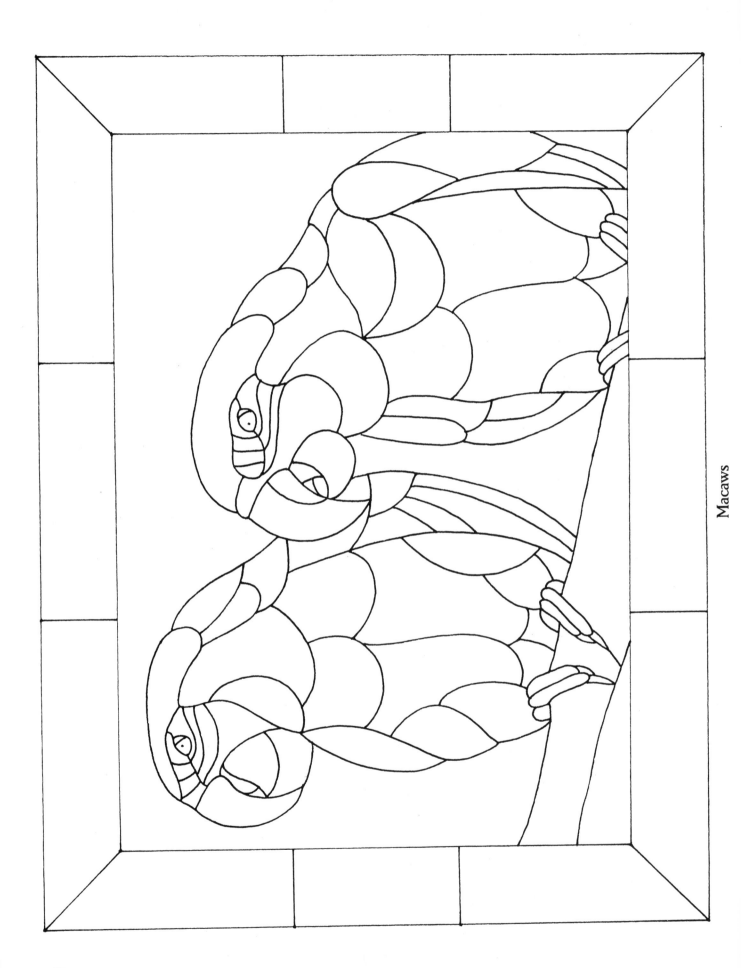

Macaws

58

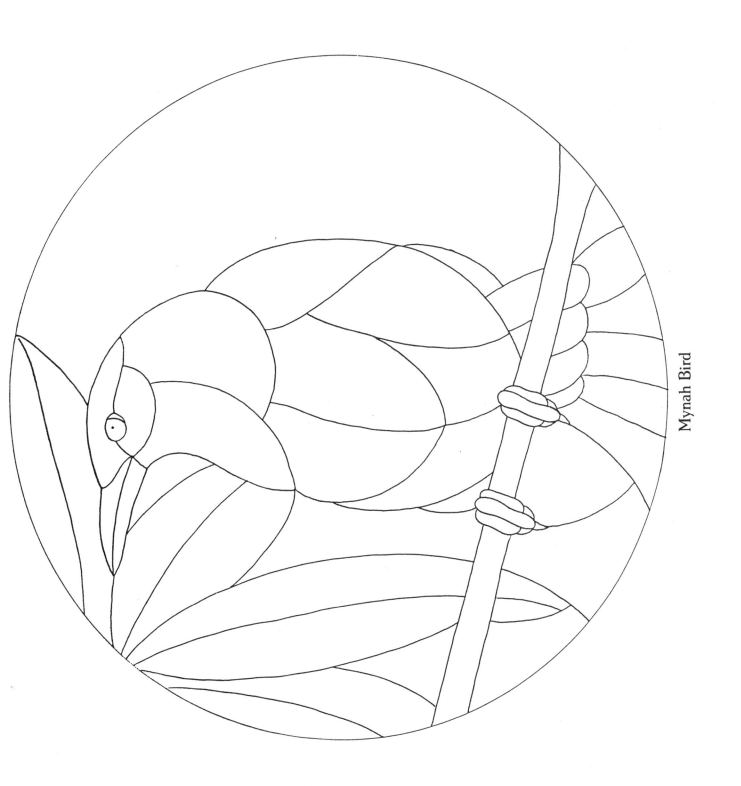

Mynah Bird

59

Masked Lovebirds